ALL QUIET ON THE WESTERN FRONT

NOTES

including
- *Life and Background of the Author*
- *General Plot Summary*
- *Remarque's Introductory Note*
- *Critical Commentaries*
- *Remarque's Style*
- *Remarque as a Social Critic*
- *Character Analyses*
- *Questions for Review*

by
Rollin O. Glaser

INCORPORATED

LINCOLN, NEBRASKA 68501

Editor	Consulting Editor
Gary Carey, M.A. *University of Colorado*	*James L. Roberts, Ph.D.* *Department of English* *University of Nebraska*

CONTENTS

ALL QUIET ON THE WESTERN FRONT NOTES

AUTHOR'S LIFE AND BACKGROUND

Erich Maria Remarque was born in Osnabrück in Westphalia, Germany, on June 22, 1898. His father, a bookbinder by trade, was German; his mother was of French descent. As a youth he attended the gymnasium (equivalent to our elementary school) and seminar in the town where he lived. While attending the University of Münster, he was drafted into the German army. He was eighteen years old at the time of his induction.

During World War I Remarque fought at the Western Front and was wounded five times, the last time seriously. Following his discharge from the army, he worked at a series of professions, all of which became the subject matter of later novels. The same "lost-ness" felt by Paul Baumer in *All Quiet on the Western Front* seems to have controlled its author in the decade following the Great War. After completing a teaching course offered by the German government to war veterans, Remarque taught school for a year in a town near the Dutch border.

His restlessness and physical energy led him to a job as a salesman for a tombstone firm. These experiences as a dealer in the "appurtenances of grief" can be found in a novel entitled *The Black Obelisk*. Having had his fill of the business world, Remarque joined a group of friends in a "gypsy caravan" touring Germany.

His wanderings temporarily completed, Remarque's future literary career gained momentum when he wrote articles for a Swiss automobile magazine and later advertising copy for the same tire company. During this period Remarque became passionately interested in automobile racing and automotive mechanics. These interests form the backdrop for his novel *Heaven Has No Favorites*.

Eventually Remarque's literary inclinations and enthusiasm for sports brought him to write *Sport im Bild*. It was at this time that *All Quiet on the Western Front* was written, the theme of which had disturbed Remarque since the war.

Published in 1928, the original manuscript had been refused by one publisher and only reluctantly accepted by another. The novel's success was immediate and overwhelming, selling almost 1½ million copies during the first year. The unusual appeal of the book is reflected in the book's first year sales by countries. German readers alone bought 800,000 copies. The United States sales were 240,000. French readers purchased 219,000 copies, and the British, 195,000 copies. It was subsequently translated and published in 25 languages. The book was later made into two different motion pictures and was equally successful in film form.

Despite its success, the book generated a storm of controversy in Germany. Some people charged that the book was "replete with effeminate pacifism;" others claimed that it was really "romantic propaganda for war." Remarque stated in an interview that these contradictory criticisms stemmed from his refusal to declare himself politically. He told one interviewer that he had been misunderstood only in those quarters where one would be misunderstood anyway. He felt no need to take part in the controversy.

Whatever political overtones the book did or did not possess have since been resolved. The novel continues to be a definitive exposé of war.

After his first successful work, Remarque devoted more of his time to writing. The following novels were written in subsequent years:

The Road Back	1931
Three Comrades	1937
Flotsam	1941
Arch of Triumph	1946

Spark of Life	1952
A Time to Love and a Time to Die	1954
The Black Obelisk	1957
Heaven Has No Favorites	1961
Night in Lisbon	1964

Because of his untenable position in Nazi Germany, Remarque went to live at Porto Ronco on Lake Maggiore in Switzerland where he later bought a house. His emigration became permanent when the Nazis came to power. Because he would not voluntarily return and continued to write critically of the Nazi party, his books were burned, his films banned, and in 1938 his citizenship was revoked.

Remarque first visited the United States in 1939. In 1947, he became an American citizen, dividing his time between New York and Switzerland.

Since the publication of *All Quiet on the Western Front*, only *Arch of Triumph*, the story of a love affair in Paris between a German refugee doctor and a Parisian actress just before the out-break of World War II, has had the same international success. Most of his works have enjoyed greater popular acclaim than critical success.

GENERAL PLOT SUMMARY

All Quiet on the Western Front is the record of seven school-mates who are representative of a generation destroyed by the shells and pressures of World War I. Because of the urgings of their teacher, Kantorek, whom they trust, all seven enlist in the army to serve the Fatherland. Paul Baumer, a young and sensitive member of the group, narrates the story.

Chapter 1

The story opens behind the German front lines. Paul and his friends are less naive as a result of their battle experience. Josef Behm has already been killed. Franz Kemmerich has had his leg amputated. A letter from Kantorek stirs the group's anger and despair at their shattered lives.

Chapter 2

The experience of military training and the war has been disillusioning for Paul and his friends. Corporal Himmelstoss wrung much of their youthful idealism out of them during basic training. The comradeship and esprit-de-corps are the only worthwhile results of their military training. At the end of the scene, Kemmerich, Paul's childhood friend, dies from his amputation.

Chapter 3

The focus in this chapter is on Kat who typifies the shrewd, self-reliant soldier. No matter what the situation, Kat is able to find food and supplies for his friends. News of Himmelstoss' arrival at the front causes Paul and his friends to remember the night before they left and how they revenged themselves on Himmelstoss.

Chapter 4

The action of this chapter is at the front. Paul and his unit have been assigned the job of laying barbed wire. While returning to the waiting trucks, Paul's company undergoes a terrific bombardment. Chapter 4 is a complete description of front-line war.

Chapter 5

Himmelstoss appears at the front and tries to make friends with Paul and his friends. He is insulted and generally abused but succeeds in having Tjaden and Kropp given light company punishment. The comradeship theme is developed further when Kat and Paul steal a goose and share it with their friends.

Chapter 6

The battle pattern described in this chapter is typical of trench warfare during World War I. Paul and his friends remain on the "line" throughout the summer and return to the rear for a rest in the fall.

Chapter 7

Paul and his comrades are moved farther behind the lines for a rest. Their time is spent eating, sleeping, and being friendly with local girls. Paul is sent home for a seventeen day leave. His homecoming is disappointing because he feels that he no longer fits or belongs. The war has destroyed his ambition and youthful pleasures. In Paul's mind the despair brought about by the war is emphasized by what he finds while on furlough.

Chapter 8

Before returning to his outfit, Paul goes through a refresher military training course at a camp on the moors. There he discovers that the men in a Russian prison camp are also human beings. This revelation further confirms doubts about the war.

Chapter 9

Returning to his unit, Paul feels the sense of belonging he was unable to feel at home. After being inspected by the Kaiser, the company is sent again to the front. In a patrol action Paul is forced to kill a French soldier named Gerard Duval. This act brings him face to face with his enemy, and he is conscience stricken by his act of murder.

Chapter 10

For three weeks Paul's squad is given the duty of guarding a supply depot. This turns out to be plush assignment, for there is an abundance of food and items of comfort. While trying to evacuate a village, Kropp and Paul are wounded. They succeed in being placed in the same hospital. Kropp's leg must be amputated. Paul recovers sufficiently to be given a leave and then returned to active duty.

Chapter 11

The action of this chapter takes place during the last summer of the war. The German war machine is crumbling, and the front line no longer exists. All of Paul's schoolmates have been killed. In this chapter Paul's best friend, Kat, is wounded, then killed by a flying splinter while being carried to a dressing station. The death of Kat is a mortal blow to Paul.

Chapter 12
The time is the fall of 1918. Paul is killed one month before the armistice on an exceptionally quiet day on the Western Front.

CHARACTERS

MAJOR CHARACTERS

Paul Baumer
The soldier, narrator and focal point of the novel who volunteered with four others from his class for military duty. Paul's group included: Muller, Kropp, Leer, Kemmerich and Behm.

Tjaden (pronounced Jahden)
A thin soldier with an immense appetite. He is nineteen and a former locksmith in civilian life.

Muller
A soldier who carries his school books with him and often dreams of examinations. He is the first to inherit Kemmerich's fine leather boots.

Stanislaus Katczinsky
Kat is a forty year old soldier who becomes Paul's best friend. He is shrewd, good-natured and known for his remarkable ability to find good food and soft jobs for the group.

Albert Kropp
First soldier of Paul's group to make lance-corporal. He was regarded as the best student in Paul's school class. He is discharged after leg amputation.

Leer
Paul's youthful classmate who grows a beard. He is first of Paul's school group to have experience with women.

Franz Kemmerich

Paul Baumer's childhood friend and fellow volunteer. Early in the novel he dies following a leg amputation. He is the first of the group to wear the fine leather boots.

Haie Westhus

The soldier who prefers the army to digging peat in civilian life.

Detering

The soldier who was a peasant-farmer in civilian life and thinks constantly of his farm and wife.

Kantorek

The schoolmaster who urged Paul and his friends to enlist. He is later called into the reserves under Mittlestaedt, a former pupil.

Corporal Himmelstoss

The drillmaster for Paul and his comrades, hated for his sadistic treatment of recruits. He is a former postman.

MINOR CHARACTERS

Josef Behm

First of Paul's schoolmates to be killed in the war.

Lieutenant Bertinck

Paul's company commander who is a fine soldier, respected by his men.

Ginger

The company cook who is more concerned about his personal safety and accurate food portions than he is concerned about feeding the men.

Tiejen

The soldier briefly recalled when Kemmerich dies. He called for his mother while dying and held off a doctor with a dagger until he collapsed.

Sergeant Oellrich
A sniper who takes pride in his ability to pick off enemy soldiers.

Heinrich Bredemeyer
A soldier who has told Paul's mother about the increasing dangers in front line fighting.

Mittelstaedt
Paul's friend who has been promoted to company commander of a home guard. He has the opportunity to take revenge on schoolmaster Kantorek who is only an ordinary soldier.

Boettcher
The soldier who was the school porter at Paul's former school.

Josef Hammacher
The soldier who shares the hospital ward with Paul, Albert and others. He has a "shooting license" because of his mental derangement.

Little Peter
One of Paul and Albert's hospital ward mates. He is thought to be the only patient ever to return from the "Dying Room."

Franz Wachter
A hospital ward mate who dies of a lung wound.

Sister Libertine
One of the sister-nurses at the hospital where Paul and Albert recover from their wounds.

Berger
The strongest soldier in Paul's company. During the last days, Berger loses his sense of judgment. He is wounded trying to rescue a messenger dog under fire.

Gerald Duval
The French soldier who lands in Paul's shell hole. Paul stabs him. After he dies, Paul discovers Duval, the enemy, is also human

—a printer with a wife and child. Paul realizes the enemy on the other side of the barbed wires is just a lonely, frightened soldier like himself.

REMARQUE'S INTRODUCTORY NOTE

All Quiet on the Western Front is prefaced by a brief statement of the novel's purpose. Here the author makes it clear that the story is not an accusation of an individual or group. It was not Remarque's intention to align himself with any particular German political party. The reader is also warned against viewing the book as an exciting adventure. This is an account of a generation of young men destroyed physically and spiritually by the experience of the war.

The book is not concerned with depicting the events of the war. The essential point is to describe war's effects on a particular generation.

It was Remarque's contention that his generation had grown up in a way different from others before and after it. Their overwhelming experience was the war. Shortly after publication of his novel, the young author declared, "The generation of young people, which no matter from what motive, has been driven through this period must necessarily have developed differently from all former generations." The men who emerged from the trenches were marked for life by deep, irreparable psychic wounds. For these young disillusioned, the world could never again hold the same innocence it had when the century was just beginning. As Jacques Barzun has put it, "The energies born with the twentieth century had been sapped, misspent and destroyed."

In a mood characterized by despair, disgust and disquiet, the youth of Europe and America returned to their private lives in 1918 to attempt to live in a world that no longer held sacred the ideals and beliefs that prevailed prior to 1914. Gertrude Stein, when she said to young Ernest Hemingway in Paris, "You are all a lost generation," summed up the dilemma Paul Baumer and his comrades would have faced had they lived.

CHAPTER 1

Summary

The novel opens behind the German front lines. What remains of Paul Baumer's company has moved back from the Western Front for a short rest after fourteen days of heavy fighting. The soldiers have been well fed. Rations for twice as many men had been prepared.

Among the mail distributed to the soldiers is a letter from Kantorek, the teacher who had persuaded Paul and his classmates to volunteer for military service. Paul comments that Kantorek is one of the little men who seem to create much of the world's unhappiness.

One of the students Kantorek succeeded in recruiting was Josef Behm. Behm was the first of Paul's schoolmates to be killed in the war. Paul realizes that Kantorek was only indirectly to blame for Behm's death, for the world is filled with men like Kantorek who must share the guilt.

Thoughts of Behm and Kantorek lead Paul to a bitter observation of the older generation. He reflects, "The idea of authority, which they represented, was associated in our minds with a greater insight and a manlier wisdom." The first bombardment and the first killing shattered this faith in the adult world. Paul and his generation feel betrayed and alone in the world they have inherited.

The second scene of the chapter focuses on Franz Kemmerich, another of Paul's comrades. Kemmerich is at a dressing station where he has just had his leg amputated. It is obvious that Kemmerich will die. Motivated by practical considerations, Muller tries unsuccessfully to persuade Kemmerich to part with his airman's boots. Muller knows that the hospital orderlies will take them as soon as Kemmerich is dead. Outside the room Kropp and his friends bribe an orderly with cigarettes to give Kemmerich morphine to ease his pain. Even with the bribe Kropp must go along to see to it that the drug is given.

The last scene of the chapter takes place back at the huts. Kropp becomes savagely angry at Kantorek's letter referring to Kropp and his friends as the "Iron Youth." Paul reflects on the word, "youth." Although none of his comrades are more than twenty, they are old, prematurely aged by the devastating experiences of war.

Commentary

The purpose of Chapter One is to establish the novel's setting, point of view, atmosphere, themes and briefly introduce the characters. Plot development is relatively unimportant in this opening chapter.

The setting is behind the German front lines during the latter part of World War I. The tide of German victories has turned, and a tired Germany now faces reinforced Allied troops. Paul Baumer, the narrator of the book, will be the character through whom you will witness the war and its effects on the other characters. Paul is typical of the young German infantry soldier who fought in the war. Although he is only twenty, he has matured beyond his years because of his experiences in the trenches. Paul's viewpoint represents the viewpoint of the author.

Note that although the story is told from the German point of view, its message is universal and representative of the thoughts and feelings of the soldiers of all of the countries that participated in the Great War. As you read through the novel, you will not be conscious of the fact that the narrative is about Germans and German action. The horror of the war belonged to all men regardless of nationality.

The general mood of a work is referred to as atmosphere. The atmosphere of this novel is pervaded by death and destruction, hopelessness and desolation. Occasionally, moments of laughter or a bit of human warmth appear unexpectedly. The light contrast sharpens one's awareness of the terrifying destruction and dangers.

The center theme of the book is the vivid portrayal of the horror and stupidity of all war. Minor themes emerge from time to time. The theft of Kemmerich's watch while at the dressing station is an example of the general decay of moral value fostered by the war. This theme will be repeated. As the novel progresses, the reader, like the hospital orderly, becomes immune to these smaller acts of immorality. The moral decline, resulting from the war, was one of the great social wounds the post war world had to attempt to heal.

CHAPTER 2

Summary

The chapter begins with Paul's thoughts about his earlier life. His present existence at the front makes memories of his youthful experiences seem vague and unreal. Because they did not have the opportunity to begin families, careers or develop strong interests, Paul and his generation feel a sense of emptiness and isolation from their society. As a result, Paul concludes that his generation has become a wasteland.

It is clear to Paul that ten years of schooling have had far less effect than ten weeks of military training. While the school attempts to teach the value of thinking, the military swiftly crushes individuality and fits people to a system. Recruits quickly discover that rank deserves more respect than wisdom.

Kropp, Muller, Kemmerich and Paul were assigned to training under the command of Corporal Himmelstoss. Himmelstoss, a mailman in civilian life, took personal satisfaction from treating recruits harshly. Because of their youthful, defiant spirit, he took a special dislike to Paul and his friends. No amount of harassment, however, could conquer their spirit, and in the end Himmelstoss was forced to give up. Paul recognizes his training as having been necessary for survival at the front. From it grew comradeship and esprit-de-corps, two positive results.

The action of the chapter takes place in Kemmerich's hospital room. It is evident from the beginning of the scene that Kemmerich is about to die. He knows that his leg has been amputated, and his pathetic statement, "I wanted to become a head-forester once," reveals that his dreams are over. Paul tries to comfort him. Kemmerich senses the nearness of his own death. Although Paul as a soldier has witnessed many deaths, his childhood friendship with Kemmerich makes this death terribly personal.

While Kemmerich is in his death throes, Paul frantically searches for a doctor. The one he finds callously refuses to be bothered, having already amputated five legs that day. Upon his return with a hospital orderly, Paul finds Kemmerich dead. Haste is made to remove him so that others outside on the floor may take his bed.

Paul's reaction to Franz Kemmerich's death is expressed in thoughts of girls, flowery meadows and white clouds—images the reverse of the death scene witnessed minutes earlier. A strong sense of his own life force pours through him. He feels a great hunger to continue living as he returns to the hut.

Commentary

Kropp's ironic statement, "We are the Iron Youth," is echoed by Paul at the beginning of this chapter. In each of the chapters, there will be at least one angry expression of disappointment with the older generation and the chaos they have caused.

One of the purposes of Chapter 2 is to give the reader an opportunity to discover more about Paul, the seeing eye of the book. He appears sensitive and intelligent. He has written poetry and attempted a play. Although his thoughts appear to be unemotional, he is capable of strong feeling and compassion as illustrated by his reaction to Kemmerich's death. His experiences with death and destruction intensify his own desire to go on living. Though Paul does not fully comprehend everything he experiences, he tries to present it as truthfully as possible. The reader will probably find himself identifying with Paul as the novel progresses. That identification is important to the success of the novel because the central message of the book is carried by Paul.

Kemmerich's death illustrates part of the central message. The event provides Remarque with the opportunity to better ask one of the questions basic to the novel: "There he lies now—but why?"

Paul then declares that the whole world ought to be forced to pass Kemmerich's deathbed so that they will say, "That is Franz Kemmerich, nineteen-and-a-half years old, he doesn't want to die. Let him not die." The scene is designed to be an object lesson to the reader. How effectively this lesson hits its mark is in part related to how well the reader has identified with Paul Baumer.

CHAPTER 3

Summary

Reinforcements for Paul's unit arrive, providing an opportunity for Paul and his friends to feel and act like "stone-age" veterans. Kropp, having a bit of fun at the expense of the newcomers, calls the new recruits, "infants." Katczinsky tells one of them that he is lucky to have bread made from turnips instead of sawdust. As a joke, Kat then offers a new recruit some haricot beans. This, of course, is taken as kidding, but true to his reputation as a clever and successful scavenger, Kat produces a stew of beef and beans.

Kat is always able to find food and supplies, no matter where he happens to be. His abilities to provide for himself and his friends are nothing short of amazing. As Paul concludes, "If for but one hour in a year something eatable were to be had in some one place only, within that hour, as if moved by a vision, (Kat) would put on his cap, go out and walk directly there, as though following a compass, and find it." His masterpiece of scrounging is four boxes of lobsters.

While relaxing and watching a dog fight between a German and an Allied plane, Kat philosophizes that if everyone in a war were given the same food and pay, the war would be over in a day. Kropp proposes that war should be staged like a full fight with entrance tickets and bands. Ministers and generals of the two countries should be armed with clubs and sent into the arena. The survivor's country wins. Kropp felt that this would prevent the wrong people from doing the fighting.

Continuing his anti-war arguments, the author uses this opportunity to discuss power in general. Kropp maintains that man is essentially a beast. He points to the difference between a man in civilian society and the same man in the army. The more insignificant a man has been in civilian life, the more power goes to his head in the military.

The action of the chapter begins with Tjaden's announcement of Himmelstoss' arrival at the front. This causes Haie Westhus, Kropp, Tjaden and Paul to recall their revenge on Himmelstoss the day before they were sent to the front. Catching Himmelstoss returning to the barracks on a dark uninhabited road, they throw a blanket over his head and beat him unmercifully. Himmelstoss never discovers his assailants' identities. Paul and his friends are later described as "young heroes" by others in the barracks. Paul's wry observation, "We had become successful students of his (Himmelstoss') methods," is one of few humorous lines in the novel.

Commentary

Although Himmelstoss' punishment satisfies the reader's sense of justice, the entire incident is further proof of Kat's observation, "In himself man is essentially a beast." The real tragedy of the matter is recognized by Paul when he points out that his group's sole ambition is to "knock the conceit out of a postman."

The purpose of the chapter is to provide the reader with a more detailed description of the men who make up Paul's unit. Chapter 2 specifically examined Paul Baumer, the narrator of the story. Chapter 3 focuses on Kat and the others. Because the viewpoint of the novel is based on the experiences of the infantry soldier, Remarque feels that it is important to give the reader a better understanding of what the ordinary soldier thinks about, talks about and feels.

The relative inaction of the chapter acts as a bridge or an interlude between Kemmerich's death and the coming chapters about the front. Chapter 4 will immerse the reader directly in the battle. Like a camera dollying in on action, the first three chapters are merely an introduction to death. The author has talked of dying. Franz Kemmerich has died a comparatively "clean" death. Now the reader must prepare to be shelled, gassed, wounded, and slaughtered.

CHAPTER 4

Summary

The action of this chapter begins just after dark one day and
ends the following morning. Paul's unit has been assigned the routine military task of laying barbed wire at the front line. Jammed
into military trucks, the soldiers are carried as far as the artillery
emplacements, just behind the front. The rest of the way must be
traveled on foot.

The air is filled with acrid smoke and the roar of artillery. The
nearness of the front brings about a change in every man. It is like
a mysterious force which each can feel. Voices sound different;
the body is in full readiness; and each man is thrown back on his
animal instincts.

At the front, rockets and bursts of flame light up the area as
Paul and the others complete their mission of rolling out and staking
down the barbed wire. While waiting for the trucks to take them
back, the men try to sleep. A sudden shelling puts an end to this.

Afterwards the air is filled with the horrible moaning of wounded horses. These sounds are especially difficult for Detering to
endure because he is a farmer and fond of horses. Finally the horses
are shot after the wounded men are treated. With the bombardment over, the men troop back toward the trucks.

The barrage starts again. Paul and his group are pinned down
in a graveyard, the only cover being mounds of earth. Suddenly the
fields become a surging sea of flame. Hit by splinters and shrapnel,
but not seriously hurt, Paul crawls toward a shell hole. In the hole
he finds a coffin and its corpse. A gas attack has started, and the
shelling makes it impossible to escape.

When the bombardment ends, the graveyard is wreckage, the
shells having unearthed the coffins and their occupants. The same
recruit Paul comforted earlier lies wounded in the stomach and hip.
It is clear to Paul and Kat that he will not live. He will be in agony

as soon as the shock wears off and for as long as he lives. They quickly agree to perform a mercy killing. Before they can act, the rest of the group gather. The situation is parallel to the scene at Kemmerich's deathbed. Kat's comment, "Young innocents—" seems to be a plea addressed to the entire world and an echo to Paul's question, "There he lies now—but why?"

Commentary

Remarque speaks of the "front" in at least two senses; as a physical location and as a psychological force. German soldiers in World War I fought on two fronts, an Eastern and a Western Front. The fighting on the Eastern Front facing Russia was mild by comparison to that on the Western Front facing France. This novel is set on the Western Front, a fighting line approximately five hundred miles long. As the war progresses, this line gradually disintegrates. Toward the end of the novel, the final breakdown can be seen in the small sector where Paul and his company are fighting.

More than just a physical location, however, the front exerted a chilling, powerful influence over the soldiers who came within its "embrace." Paul describes the front as a "mysterious whirlpool" whose vortex he can feel sucking him "slowly, irresistibly and inescapably into itself." Moreover, this influence can be felt at some distance. As soon as Paul and his unit reach the artillery lines, the men feel it in their veins, in their hands, and there is "...a tense waiting, a watching, a profound growth, a strange sharpening of the senses..." It often seems to Paul that the air at the front shudders and vibrates, emitting an electric current of its own.

Chapter Four provides the reader some clear insights into the nature of World War I. Except for the naval battle of Jutland, this was mainly a land war. The trench became the soldier's home while at the front. Intricate tunnel networks were constructed by both sides. Paul acknowledges this basic relationship between earth and soldier when he states, "To no man does the earth mean so much as to the soldier." Later, Paul's reflections about the earth have a hymn-like quality. "Earth!—Earth!—Earth!" he chants. She is the soldier's only friend, his brother, and his mother. She may give him a new lease on life for another ten seconds, or she may receive him forever.

Continuing the development of the earth theme, the final scene of the chapter takes place in a cemetery. This place of death appropriately emphasizes the life-death existence of the soldier. During the shelling the relationship between the living and the dead becomes intimate. The living crawling into coffins with the dead to escape the bombardment. Paul points out that each of the dead that was flung up from a grave saved one of the soldiers. Finally, the living-dead theme is used to describe the state of the exhausted soldiers as they ride in the trucks back to the huts.

Remarque's use of horses in this chapter serves several purposes. (1) The presence of animals in the midst of battle dates the war. World War I was the beginning of modern mechanized warfare. Trucks, tanks, airplanes, and other modern weapons were in their early stages of development. Horses and donkeys were used extensively at the beginning of the war.

(2) The majestic bearing of the animals provides another contrast to the foolish, wretched activities of men. Just before moving into the front lines to lay the barbed wire, Paul encounters a column of men and horses. The horses are strangely beautiful as their backs shine in the moonlight and they toss their heads. The whole procession reminds Paul of a line of knights and their steeds. Later, however, after a bombardment, the same horses are wounded and dying. Their cries are terrible and unearthly. Some gallop into the distance, guts trailing in the dust, reminding one of the unfortunate horses used in bull fights.

(3) Paul comments that the sound of the dying horses is like the "moaning of the world...martyred creation, wild with anguish, filled with terror and groaning." It is as if all of creation has risen to accuse Man.

If you have ever wondered how an author creates a climax or moves a reader to a fevered pitch in a fictional account, this chapter is an excellent illustration. Beginning with the placid entry to the front lines and ending with the horror of horrors, the shelling in the graveyard, the selection of detail is deliberate and dramatic. Each is calculated to move the reader to a more intense emotional level. Notice the constant appeal to the senses: the color of the flares and rockets, the sounds emitted by all sizes of shells and bullets, the moaning of the dying horses, the cries of wounded men, the sense of suffocation felt when a man wears a gas mask after the air has been used up. All of these carefully placed details contribute to the impact of one of the most vivid chapters in the whole novel.

CHAPTER 5

Summary
    Following the laying of barbed wire at the front, the soldiers in Paul's company are returned to the huts behind the lines. Time is passed in killing lice and anticipating the arrival of Himmelstoss, the harsh drillmaster.

While discussing Himmelstoss' reception, Muller poses a question often mused upon by the battle weary soldier: "What would you do if peace were declared tomorrow?" Each soldier in the group gives a different answer, representative of the spectrum of typical responses. Answers range from Haie Westhus' wish to remain in the peacetime army because it is better than digging peat for a living to Tjaden's vengeful desire to spend the rest of his life torturing Himmelstoss. The conclusion of the discussion is representative of the conclusion reached by the youth in German and Allied armies. Much of the trivial information drilled in the classroom had no practical application in the trenches.

Kropp expresses the feeling of the group when he says, "The war has ruined us for everything." It has squelched all ambition to become anything. Paul summarizes this loss when he concludes: "We don't want to take the world by storm. We are fleeing. We fly from ourselves. From our life. We were eighteen and had begun to love life and the world; and we had to shoot it to pieces. The first bomb, the first explosion burst in our hearts. We are cut off from activity, from striving, from progress. We believe in such things no longer, we believe in the war."

During the discussion Himmelstoss appears. The situation is reversed, and now Himmelstoss is the green new arrival. Insulted by Tjaden, Himmelstoss stalks off to the orderly room to have him arrested. The company commander, Lieutenant Bertinck, is sympathetic to Paul and his friends, but he is bound by duty to punish insubordination. Tjaden and Kropp are given light sentences of "open arrest."

The chapter ends with an episode in which Kat and Paul roast a stolen goose. Sitting together in the darkened hut, sharing the food and comradeship, they are described as "two minute sparks of life; outside is the night and the circle of death." The brotherhood that springs forth when men face a common danger is the only positive result of the war. The remaining food is shared with Kropp and Tjaden at the compound, and the circle of friendship is enlarged.

Commentary

One of the important laws of drama (and fiction) has to do with the use of contrast. Prudently used, contrasting scenes heighten the effect of essential scenes or those which advance the main action of the plot. Remarque purposively places scenes in the novel to produce the maximal emotional effect on the reader. Chapter 4 immersed the reader in the hell of warfare. Chapter 5 is relaxed and relatively free from the horror of the war. This is the pattern Remarque uses, his theory being that only through the hell of war can a man realize the absolute sweetness of peace. Again in Chapter 6, the reader is moved with Paul and his friends up to the front line to face an assault of the French troops. And so it goes all through the novel. Sometimes the contrast will be effected within a chapter, as in Chapter 6 when Paul dreams of childhood scenes after a bloody attack.

The purpose of Chapter 5 is to provide a relief from the action of Chapters 4 and 6. Two themes are developed further: the loss of ambition brought about by the war; the brotherhood that life in the trenches fostered.

CHAPTER 6

Summary

The action of this chapter is typical of the trench warfare of World War I. An offensive commonly began with a prolonged artillery bombardment. An infantry attack would follow. This usually forced a withdrawal to a second line of defense where the attack would be repulsed. A counter-attack would carry the battle back to the enemy front lines. Finally, both sides would return to their original positions. So it went throughout most of the war, the Western Front line remained relatively stable despite great loss of life.

Remarque sets the scene for a typical slaughter with a high, double wall of new coffins. Ironically, these mute symbols of death are stacked against a shelled schoolhouse, another symbol of Paul's former life.

Paul describes the front as a kind of "cage" in which everyone must fearfully wait for whatever may happen. Staying alive is recognized by every soldier as a matter of pure chance. The action of this chapter makes this perfectly clear.

The approaching offensive is signaled by the prevalence of corpse-rats, extra rations, increased supplies of ammunition, and rumors about new enemy weapons. Day after day the heavy bombardment continues until there is little left of the trench system. The tension caused by waiting for the attack drives many of the green recruits to madness.

When the attack finally comes, Paul and the others are transformed into animals defending themselves against annihilation. It is not fighting, but self-preservation that motivates the soldier in the midst of a fierce battle. Paul sums up the soldier's will to survive when he says, "If your own father came over with them you would not hesitate to fling a bomb into him."

The holocaust seethes and grows, gaining momentum like a charging steed until Remarque reaches the ultimate in descriptions of front line horrors—"men living with their skulls blown open... soldiers running with their two feet cut off..." and so on and bloodily on. The death of Kemmerich early in the novel seems cheerful by comparison. The battle subsides after the loss of a few hundred yards and many hundreds of lives.

Following a summer of this kind of fighting, the remaining thirty-two men out of 150 in Paul's company return to the rear lines.

Commentary

Chapter 6 focuses on the characteristic pattern of world War I front line battle. Remarque tries to demonstrate the futility of wholesale slaughter for the purpose of gaining a few yards of worthless earth. Rather than simply telling the reader that war is hell, which most people agree to intellectually, the author forces us to see and feel the experience from the viewpoint of the infantryman. No holds are barred in this chapter, as none should be. The sharpened spade and the saw tooth bayonet are examples of the terrible brutalities of this war. The horrors are endless, and Remarque makes this chapter more grim, more repugnant than any of the preceding. By the end of it, the reader has become numb to human suffering, a condition roughly akin to that possessed by the veteran after long exposure to death.

In contrast to the images of destruction in this chapter, there are many references to children and images of beauty and innocence. One morning, for example, Paul watches two butterflies at play in front of his trench. They offer a brilliant contrast to the stark, shell-torn landscape. Again in the next chapter Paul contemplates butterflies, but they are the ones he caught as a child. The butterflies serve both to contrast with Paul's present existence and to symbolize his lost childhood.

Paul sees his own childhood reflected in the young recruits sent to the front, poorly trained and outfitted in uniforms never intended for childish measurements. Between five and ten recruits are killed for every experienced soldier. The presence of these very young replacements was indicative of a crumbling Germany which had reached the bottom of her manpower barrel.

The image of forlorn children is used again to convey the feelings of Paul's generation. "We are forlorn like children, and experienced like old men, we are crude and sorrowful and superficial — I believe we are lost." The reference to the lost generation of the twenties is clearly intended.

CHAPTER 7

Summary

Chapter 7 consists of three basic scenes; the first two provide a transition to the most important scene, Paul's experience with his family and friends at home on leave.

Because two-thirds of his company were killed or wounded, Paul's unit is taken to a field depot where they are given an abundance of food and rest. Here the terror of the front is temporarily forgotten. The soldiers are even able to joke about their experiences, but this is really only a way to keep from thinking seriously about them. Paul knows that there will come a time when all of these memories will return to haunt those who survive.

An old movie poster with the figure of a pretty girl and a young man in white trousers reminds Paul and Albert Kropp that there is another side to life. While swimming, Paul and his friends strike up an acquantance with three enemy French women who live across the sentry-guarded river. By promising food, Tjaden and the others are able to arrange a rendezvous for that evening. The evening meetings continue until Paul receives a seventeen day leave, after which he must report to the moors for a training course before returning to his company.

The train ride home prepares Paul for his old life as he sees a panorama of meadows, farms, children and finally his own home town. The trip from the station to his home is filled with places and memories of childhood experiences. The transition from front to home is completed when Paul hears the voice of his own sister and sobs.

Early in his visit Paul finds that a distance has grown between him and his family. The change is not so much in the family as it is in Paul. Even his room and books, which were so painstakingly collected, fail to stir his former interest and ambition. Having not directly experienced the war, the people Paul meets have no real understanding of the German predicament. His old German master refers to Paul as a "young warrior" and talks of a breakthrough and final victory.

While on leave Paul visits Mittelstaedt, a former school companion who has been promoted to company commander. Kantorek, the teacher responsible for recruiting Paul and his classmates for the military, has been assigned to Mittelstaedt's company as an ordinary soldier. Mittelstaedt takes every opportunity to torment him. He taunts Kantorek with his own valiant phrases, ordering him to perform the most menial tasks. Boettcher, the former school porter, is a model soldier in the company. During his last four days, Paul pays a visit to Franz Kemmerich's mother. To assuage her grief, he is forced to invent a story and swear that her son's death was instantaneous and that he felt no pain.

When his leave is over, Paul can only conclude that his stay at home has made matters worse. Before coming home he was indifferent and hopeless. Now he is in agony for himself, for his mother who is dying of cancer, and for his lost youth.

Commentary

The technical handling of this chapter is worth a brief analysis. Artistically Remarque faces the difficult problem of orientating the reader from the battlefront to the homefront. The transition is made gradually by removing Paul's unit farther behind the lines, introducing a poster with the fresh, young girl who suggests a forgotten side of life, providing an episode involving Paul and his comrades with three French girls, and finally describing the familiar countryside and home town as it appears to Paul during his journey home. Within a few pages the reader scarcely realizes that he is now being presented with a scene offering the most important contrast in the novel.

The rest of the chapter is devoted to Paul's recognition of the changes that have taken place within himself as a result of his war experiences. The magnitude of the change is made clear when Paul puts on his civilian clothes. "I feel awkward," he says. "The suit is rather tight and short. I have grown in the army." The growth must be understood in a double sense, having direct reference to changes in Paul's inner life as reflected by a later comment, "...now I saw that I have been crushed without knowing it. I find I do not belong here any more, it is a foreign world." Like so many of his generation, Paul was irreconcilably isolated from his former life. Because leave only made him more acutely aware of this isolation, Paul concludes that coming home was a mistake.

In this chapter the reader can see a partial reason for the writing and teaching of this book. None of the home people show any real understanding of this specific war and the efforts of war in general. Consider the advice Paul's mother gives him: watch out for French girls and be careful at the front. Paul's father wants to hear of his son's war adventures. Former teachers talk of victory. The novel then is an attempt to dramatize the bitter truth.

CHAPTER 8

Summary

A military training camp on the moors provides the setting for Chapter 8. The camp is near enough to Paul's home so that his sister and father can visit him on a Sunday afternoon. Paul's days are occupied by routine company drill. Evenings are spent at the Soldier's Home, a place for relaxation when off duty, and a place where Paul can play the piano. The atmosphere of the camp is relaxed and undemanding. Paul makes no close friends, preferring to being alone with his thoughts. Many of his reflections concern nature. The fall colors and peace of the moors make the war seem remote.

Next to the training camp is a Russian prisoner-of-war camp. Because of the general scarcity of food, the prisoners are on the verge of starving to death. They are a docile, pathetic lot, spending much of their time searching the garbage for scraps of food. To obtain additional food, the Russians trade their personal belongings or carved trinkets, but the German peasants drive a hard bargain.

Daily contact with the prisoners causes Paul to reflect on the fact that a word of command has made these people his enemies. An unseen document has legalized mass murder. Paul is frightened by his own thoughts, but vows to give them further consideration when the war is over. He vaguely understands that he will crusade against war and spread the truth and that this task will be the only one that will make life worthy after the hideous years in the trenches.

Paul is visited by his sister and father on the last Sunday before he is to return to the front. It is a depressing, uncomfortable visit. He learns that his mother has gone to the hospital because of cancer and will be operated on shortly. Family funds are inadequate. Paul knows that his father will have to put in many hours of overtime to pay for the operation. When his father and sister leave, they give him some food from home which he shares with the Russian prisoners.

Commentary

Throughout the novel Paul continually makes discoveries about society and about himself. It must be remembered that Paul is young, his thinking has not matured, and that he is groping towards the truth. His thoughts about the Russian prisoners, for example lead him to some frightening conclusions, frightening because they contradict what he has been taught by the society in which he lives. "I dare think this way no more. This way lies the abyss," he concludes when he discovers that the Russians are really human beings like his own countrymen. At the same time Paul becomes aware of a vague obligation to tell the world of this revelation. He sees his future role in society as one where he spreads this truth. Interestingly enough, this is exactly how Remarque has spent the rest of his life. His stories change, but the themes are always the same.

CHAPTER 9

Summary

After several nights of searching for his unit, Paul finds that they have been designated the "flying division" to be used wherever the battle is heaviest. Reunited finally with Kat and the others, Paul feels a sense of homecoming and belongingness.

In preparation for an inspection by the Kaiser, new uniforms are issued. Everything is cleaned and polished for the coming review. Paul is disappointed when the Kaiser appears, having had the impression that his voice was deeper and that he was taller. The visit, however, generates another discussion of the causes of the war. Paul and his friends find it difficult to understand how both sides can be fighting for a just cause. One must be in error. Again the point is made that the participants in the war are ordinary people like themselves who would prefer to be leading peaceful lives at home. The real causes of the war are incomprehensible to the common man, and in the end he can only conclude that there is the front and he is there and that is that.

Paul's company is again sent to the front although there had been a rumor that they were to be sent to Russia. While on patrol, Paul becomes panicky and temporarily loses his courage. Hearing the voices of his friends talking in the trenches, he is calmed and feels a sense of identity with his comrades.

Later, on the same patrol, Paul loses his sense of direction and is pinned down in a shell hole during an enemy attack. Face down in the mud, he pretends to be dead as the first wave of troops pass over him. When the attack is repulsed, a retreating French soldier jumps into his shell hole to escape the German machine gun fire. Striking blindly, Paul stabs the man with his dagger. Throughout the next day Paul is forced to remain in the shell hole with the mortally wounded soldier. During this time the soldier gasps for air and looks terrorized at Paul when he tries to bandage his wounds and give him water. About three in the afternoon, the French soldier dies.

Wishing it had been otherwise, Paul is stricken by his conscience. The war has suddenly become terribly personal for Paul. Later he identifies the soldier as Gerard Duval, a printer with a wife and a child. In a moment of emotional agony, Paul vows to make amends to the man's family, to spend the rest of his life preventing the occurrence of another such war.

When it becomes dark again, Paul returns to his lines. The next morning he relates the incident to Kat and Albert. They assure him that it is not his fault and that he did the only thing he could. Above them at a firing stand, Sergeant Oellrich deliberately snipes at the enemy, taking pride and pleasure from picking off human lives. He will receive an award for having a high score. Observing this, Paul attempts to justify his killing of Duval by saying, "After all, war is war." This is an attempt to ease his stricken conscience.

Commentary

The most important value Paul finds in his life as a soldier is the comradeship with the men in his unit. But for these single human relationships, he might have been driven to madness. Two examples of the importance of this comraderie are found in this chapter. When Paul returns from his leave and training camp, he breathes a great sigh of relief and says simply, "This is where I belong." His return to camp is far more meaningful to him than his return home on leave. A second example occurs when Paul is on patrol and suddenly loses his control and courage. Hearing the voices of his own troops and thinking he hears the voice of Kat is enough to calm him and help him regain his composure. "I am no longer a shuddering speck of existence, alone in the darkness... we are nearer than lovers...," he comments. These friendships are the only solid elements of the soldier's life.

In the previous chapter Remarque placed Paul near a camp of Russian prisoners. Here he discovered that these creatures were human that they "look just as kindly as our peasants in Friesland." This experience leads Paul to see the war in more personal and human terms. Before this it had been a matter of ducking enemy shells and firing back from a great distance. The enemy remained faceless. Murdering him was a reasonable front line behavior. In this chapter Remarque deliberately brought Paul face to face with an enemy who suddenly has a name, a family, a past and dreams. He turns out to be an ordinary man—a printer by trade —a man who writes his wife each day and has a little girl. In a soliloquy after Duval's death, Paul asks, "Why do they never tell us that you are just poor devils like us, that your mothers are just as anxious as ours and that we have the same fear of death, and the same dying and the same agony—Forgive me, comrade; how could you be my enemy?"

After this experience, Paul's comment that war is war is only a half-believed statement—a mask for his real feeling which he still only partially understands.

CHAPTER 10

Summary
Paul's squad has been selected to guard the supply depot of an otherwise abandoned village. From the town's shell torn houses, they provision themselves with food and the comforts of home. For three weeks they glut themselves with food and sleep while the town is gradually leveled by shells.

A few days after this assignment, Albert Kropp and Paul are caught in the open, trying to evacuate a village. Both are wounded, Paul in the leg and arm and Albert in the leg. They are picked up by an ambulance and taken to a dressing station. There an army surgeon cruelly and unnecessarily probes Paul's wound.

By bribing a sergeant-major with cigars left over from the supply depot, Albert and Paul are able to get themselves placed on a hospital train returning to the rear lines. While on the train Albert's fever begins to rise, and he is in danger of being separated from Paul. By heating his temperature thermometer, Paul is able to pretend that he too has a fever, and both succeed in being put off at the same station.

Paul and Albert are placed in the same room in a Catholic hospital. Here they meet Josef Hammacher, who has a "shooting license" certificate saying that he is not to be held responsible for his actions; Franz Wachter, who later dies of a lung wound; and little Peter, the only patient ever to return from the "Dying Room," a place where patients who are about to die are sent.

Many patients come and go in Paul and Albert's room. Paul's bones will not knit, and they operate on him. Albert's leg is amputated. On recovery, Albert is sent to an institute for artifical limbs, Paul is given another leave, before he returns to the front lines.

Commentary

At this point in the development of the novel, it is appropriate for Remarque to devote an entire chapter to a tour of a wartime hospital. Working backward from the author's summary comment, "A hospital alone shows what war is," observe the presentation of details in this chapter. The opening scene, relatively happy, does not prepare you for what is to follow. Even the continual removal of wounded to the "Dying Room" does not pack much of a wallop in view of previous combat descriptions. When Paul is able to walk around the hospital, Remarque has opportunity to detail all of the various wounds and their consequences. It is so staggering that Paul at first can only comment, "Here a man realizes for the first time in how many places a man can get hit." To complete the calculated effect, Remarque then asks the reader to bear in mind that he is describing only one hospital and that there are hundreds of thousands in Germany and France and Russia. Clearly, one need go no further than the nearest military hospital to have a complete experience of what war is like.

All of this, of course, leads Paul to two questions: what is the logic of a thousand-year culture that permits these torture chambers? What is to become of my generation now that my knowledge of life is limited to death? These two questions are at the core of the novel.

The medical profession in this chapter is dealt a blow. Doctors seem cruel, interested in using patients for guinea pigs to further their own experimentation, and preferring amputation to surgical repair because it is easier. As Josef Hammacher put it, "...the war is a glorious time...for all the surgeons." Remarque exploits the example of the chief surgeon's experiments in correcting flat feet. He produces club feet instead. No doubt there was truth to these examples, yet the pressure of mass operations, inadequate supplies and personnel, and poor conditions for treatment of patients must have compounded the problem enormously.

CHAPTER 11

Summary

Chapter 11 records the final collapse of the German army and the Western Front. It also records the deaths of all of Paul's comrades, Muller, Bertinck, Leer and finally Kat.

Life for the soldier alternates between the front and the rest camps. The men are reduced to "unthinking animals," and only their strong sense of camaraderie helps them to endure their condition.

Detering sees a cherry tree in blossom in a garden. He is so deeply affected by memories of his own farm that he deserts and tries to go home. He is caught and court-martialed. The case of Detering is typical of the general madness overtaking the men.

Outnumbered, underfed, without supplies, the army continues to fight. Weapons newly discovered and invented at the beginning of the war, became perfected by the end of it. Tanks, planes and flame throwers are now brought in by Allied troops in abundance. As Paul puts it, there is no escape but the trench, the hospital or the grave.

Kat's shin is smashed by a bullet. Paul carries him on his back to a dressing station. Near the station Kat catches a splinter in his head. He is dead on arrival. This is the final blow for Paul.

Commentary

The main purpose of this chapter is to complete the destruction of Paul's inner life. The death of his best friend, Kat, is really the end of Paul's life. When his actual death comes in the next chapter, it is difficult to feel a sense of loss. Paul has depended on his comrades for a shred of security. One by one they have been killed. The death of Kat is the final blow that strips Paul of everything resembling human comfort.

This chapter also records the entry of America into the war, bringing with her fresh men and supplies and hurling them against an exhausted Germany. Everything goes to pieces in this chapter — even the front crumbles as the troops are reduced to crater warfare. The Germans bring up very young soldiers who only know how to die.

For those who have survived the war to this point, there is the sickening fear that death will come just before it's all over. Stephen Crane's short story, "The Open Boat," expresses the feeling of the German soldier during the last days of the summer of 1918: "If I am going to be drowned — if I am going to be drowned — if I am going to be drowned, why, in the name of the seven mad gods who rule sea, was I allowed to come thus far and contemplate sand and trees?" Paul is killed one month before the Armistice.

Two items in this chapter offer an excellent opportunity to observe the interaction of symbols and narrative: the cherry blossoms and the boots. The blossoms, of course, suggest spring, a of rebirth and life. For the farmer, spring is a time for planting and nurturing life. Detering, faced daily with death, goes suddenly mad when he encounters the fact and symbol of spring in the midst of the shell torn landscape of the front. The memory and attraction of spring is too great for him to resist. He follows his inner calling to his farm and spring plowing. In a sense, the tree was a call to life for Detering — a last chance to escape the perpetual winter and death of the front. It is small wonder that Detering responded.

The boots are woven like a thread throughout the novel. Kemmerich first possesses them, but even he got them from an airman. They are passed to Muller who gives them to Paul who promises them to Tjaden. In a sense the boots serve to unite the friends, being passed and worn by each in turn.

CHAPTER 12

Summary

It is the fall of 1918, and Paul is the only one of the seven classmates remaining. There is a great deal of talk about peace, and revolution is threatened if it does not come.

Paul has been given a fourteen day rest because of gas poisoning. He again reflects on the fate of his generation and his personal destiny. His prediction is that his generation is without hope and will fall to ruin because of the destruction of its spirit.

The last two paragraphs are written in the third person in the form of an epitaph or epilogue. Paul Baumer was killed one month before the Armistice. He fell "on a day that was so quiet and still on the whole front, that the army report confined itself to the single sentence: All quiet on the Western Front."

Commentary

The death of Paul is an anticlimax. The emotion experienced by the reader is probably a general feeling in response to the novel as a whole rather than specifically to Paul's death. Had he survived the war, he would have joined the frustrated, searching group of adults who were appropriately referred to as the Lost Generation of the Twenties.

The ideas expressed by Paul in the final chapter are a repetition of those voiced throughout the novel.

THE AUTHOR'S STYLE

With the exception of the last two paragraphs of the novel, *All Quiet on the Western Front* is written in the first person narrative point of view. As used in this novel, the first person has both advantages and disadvantages. It is a definite advantage to the author to use a method of telling his story that will force the reader to identify with the thoughts and conclusions of the main character. Use of the first person gives the impression of actual experience being transmitted to the reader without the usual interference from the mind of a third party.

On the other side of the coin, Paul, our narrator, is young and immature. We are asked to consider and accept some rather momentous conclusions based on the experience of a ninteen year old infantry soldier. In the case of this novel, however, the advantages of the first person point of view far outstrip the disadvantages. What Paul does not have in years is more than accounted for in what the reader interprets as honesty and devotion to a principle which transcends any national allegiance.

The outstanding feature of Remarque's style lies in his sense of the theatrical. Each of the twelve chapters in the book is carefully placed so that the subject of each draws the reader closer to the important conclusion Remarque wishes him to reach. By using contrasting scenes and chapters, the reader is paced so that individual scenes will produce the greatest possible effect. All this is lighted with the glare of rockets and flares, complete with the sound effects of shells, men and animals.

Coupled with Remarque's ability to handle description, images and symbols, the novel transcends ordinary battlefield fiction. Paul and friends come to life. The truth they speak is not limited to a single war in a century of wars.

REMARQUE AS A SOCIAL CRITIC

With firm belief in an early and complete military victory, both sides entered the First World War. Nine million lives and four wasted empires later, the great conflict ended. The cost in human life and property was staggering: 22 million were wounded, 7 million of them were permanently disabled; over 9 million civilians were killed. A total cost of 400 billion dollars financed the holocaust.

Could they have been reckoned, the hidden costs probably would have been even greater. The damage to a generation of men on both sides was inestimable. In a sense, *All Quiet on the Western Front* is a firsthand account of this "hidden cost" of war. Remarque, himself a front line soldier who experienced all he wrote of, seethed with despair and unrest for ten years before he brought himself to write his reactions.

The success of this first novel was immediate and enormous. A journalist for the Boston *Evening Transcript* reported that within the first year almost 1½ million copies of the book were printed and that 800,000 alone were sold in Germany. Clearly, Remarque's short novel, dramatizing the war experiences of a young German foot soldier, touched the heart of the matter for people on both sides of the Atlantic who ten years later still deeply felt the experience of the war.

It can only be concluded that Remarque was in tune with the general feeling of his generation and his times and that he was able to communicate this tragic event with honesty, precision and clarity.

Although the book is an account of World War I from the viewpoint of an ordinary soldier, the criticism of the German war machine and the Kaiser is apparent. In the beginning of the novel, and repeated in every chapter at least once, is a tirade against the boastful supremacy of German nationalism ideas preached by the elder, supposedly responsible members of society. It was this inflated viewpoint that was responsible for bringing the Behm's and the Kemmerich's into the military and up to the front where they quickly became cannon fodder. The guardians of the society — the teachers, the government, the military, the elders — conspired knowingly and unknowingly to nurture the myth of German supremacy. The falsity of this notion was revealed, as Paul puts it, when the first explosion came and the first of his schoolmates fell in battle.

The same disastrous nationalism could be seen growing again during the twenties and thirties. The bitter lesson of defeat had not really been learned. Remarque and others could see the mistakes of the Kaiser and the German Republic about to be repeated under Hitler's leadership.

In addition to his criticism of contemporary Germany, Remarque poses some penetrating questions regarding the very nature of Man. Contrasted to the animals in some of the scenes of the novel, Man looks foolish and shabby. Just before moving into the front lines to lay barbed wire, Paul encounters a column of men and horses. The horses are strangely beautiful as they toss their heads in the moonlight. The whole procession reminds Paul of a line of knights and their steeds. Later, after a severe bombardment, the same horses are wounded and dying. Their cries are terrible and unearthly. Some gallop into the distance, their entrails dragging in the dust. Paul comments that the sound of the dying horses is like the "moaning of the world...martyred creation wild with anguish, filled with terror and groaning." It is as if all of creation has risen to accuse Man, the great destroyer.

Despite the serious nature of Remarque's insights into both Man and Society, the tone of the novel is restrained and not overwhelmingly bitter. As a result, the emotional impact of the novel on the reader is apt to be great – perhaps greater than that felt after reading all subsequent books on war.

MAJOR CHARACTER ANALYSES

Paul Baumer

Paul Baumer is the character through whose eyes the reader views the action and thought of the novel. Through Paul, the author speaks of his experiences and reaction to the First World War.

Paul is typical of the young German infantry soldier who is brought to the front lines after a brief period of training. His growth to manhood is completed amid the wretchedness and despair of those who fight and died in the trenches.

At the time the story opens, Paul, although only twenty years old, is already a hardened veteran. One of his schoolmates, Josef Behm has been killed. Another, Franz Kemmerich will die shortly from a leg amputation. Most of Paul's youthful idealism, learned in school and fostered by his parents and teachers, has disappeared. Although he accepts his lot as a front line soldier, he becomes increasingly aware of the futility of the war and its colossal waste of human life.

Paul does not undergo a major character change during the novel. Much of the real destruction of his ambition and ideals has occurred before the first chapter begins. The subsequent action of the story sees this destruction completed as his few remaining values and hopes are shattered. His friends are killed, his past becomes meaningless, and he has no future. His net gain is a few fundamental truths about war and society. Beyond this Paul is emotionally and intellectually bankrupt.

Corporal Himmelstoss

Himmelstoss, the corporal responsible for the basic training given to Paul Baumer and his comrades, typifies the truism that power corrupts. Himmelstoss, a little man, uses his petty authority over recruits to satisfy his personal desire for power. A postman in civilian life, he takes every opportunity to make life miserable for green army recruits. Paul and his friends finally get their revenge, but only a front line shelling has any real effect on Himmelstoss' character.

Himmelstoss represents a military type universally hated and feared. A few stripes or insignia make these individuals tyrants of their own small worlds.

Stanislaus Katczinsky

Although not one of Paul's classmates, Katczinsky becomes Paul's closest friend. He is forty years old and a cobbler by trade. Their differences in age and background only serve to draw Katczinsky and Paul closer together. Called Kat by his friends, he has the uncanny ability to find food and the comforts of home in places where not so much as a crust of bread is available. Kat symbolizes the shrewd, self-reliant soldier who has turned his imagination and inventiveness to practical uses.

Above all Kat is warm and good natured. His death near the close of the war is the final shock for Paul. Kat is the last and best of his friends.

Kantorek

Kantorek is the teacher who persuaded Paul and his classmates to assume their patriotic responsibilities and enlist in the army. He uses his position as a teacher to spread the myth of the German Destiny. For Paul and his friends, Kantorek represents the betrayal of youth by the older generation.

Later Kantorek is called up as a reservist and placed in a unit under the command of Mittlestaedt, a former pupil. The situation provides Mittlestaedt with an unlimited opportunity to inflict all of the indignities on his former teacher which he had suffered as a former student. The pattern of revenge parallels that taken on Himmelstoss. The two situations indicate the loss of esteem suffered by the elder generation.

Albert Kropp

Albert Kropp is one of Paul's classmates. He has a reputation for being the best thinker in Paul's class. In group discussions, Kropp proposes the most profound solutions to problems. It is his idea, for example, to transform the institution of war into a kind of public festival held in an arena. Only the politicians and generals can be injured while the common man simply watches and awaits the outcome.

Both Albert Kropp and Paul Baumer are sent to a military hospital behind the lines because of wounds. Kropp's leg is amputated, and he is eventually sent home. He presumably survives the war, although he is not mentioned again.

Tjaden

He is described as skinny and having a sharp, mousy appearance. Nonetheless, Tjaden is the most voracious eater in Paul's company. He is like a growing adolescent who is never filled. The reader first meets Tjaden as he is ready to pick a fight with Ginger, the company cook, who appears to be welching on rations ordered for a full complement of soldiers. Because of heavy casualties, only a part of the company has returned for chow. This causes a super-abundance of food. Tjaden sees this overage as rightfully belonging to him and the men remaining. Ginger is concerned because he has overdrawn. Each views the food in his characteristic manner, Ginger as a miser and Tjaden as a glutton.

Tjaden was not one of Paul's classmates. He was of the same age as the others and fits well in the group with Kropp, Muller and the others. In civilian life he had worked as a locksmith.

Detering

Detering is an example of the simple, peace-loving peasant farmer who cared more for his wife and farm than political philosophies and militarism. He spends most of his time dreaming of tilling the soil and harvesting crops. One spring when nature surrounds him with memories of his home, he becomes deranged and goes A.W.O.L. His desire to return to his farm is so strong that all caution and reason are ignored. He is caught and court martialed.

Haie Westhus

In private life Haie Westhus was a digger of peat, a job that would be comparable to that of a coal miner. For Haie, the peace-time army seems attractive. It offers him a clean place to sleep, three square meals and a cleaner job. Haie is the only one in Paul's group who would reenlist in the postwar army if given the opportunity.

QUESTIONS

1. What is the significance of the statement, "To no man does the earth mean so much as the soldier?"

2. How does the author's use of contrasting scenes make the novel's ideas more vivid and forceful?

3. Consider the actions of Paul's family and friends when he is home on leave. How do these individual situations illustrate the public's lack of understanding of the war?

4. Has Remarque fulfilled his purpose as set forth in the preface to the book? Illustrate your conclusion with examples from the book.

5. Contrast Paul's killing of Gerard Duval with Sergeant Oellrich's sniping at the enemy at the front. Wherein lies the difference in their actions?

6. What was Remarque's opinion of the medical profession during the war? Does this opinion appear to be justified?

7. The death of the main character provides the climax to the plot structure in many novels. Why isn't this true of *All Quiet on the Western Front?* Where is the climax of this novel?

SUGGESTED THEME TOPICS

1. Many of Germany's postwar problems are intimated in the novel. After reading Remarque's, *The Road Back,* trace the relationship of the problems in both novels.

2. Compare the emotional and intellectual growth of Paul Baumer to some other anti-war protagonist such as Henry Fleming in *The Red Badge of Courage,* the youthful foot soldier in Civil War battles.

3. Compare the overall effect of *All Quiet on the Western Front* with another literary form that develops the same basic theme. Wilfred Owen's poem, "Dulce Et Decorum Est" might offer a good comparison.

Here's a Great Way to Study Shakespeare and Chaucer.

Complete study Edition

Hamlet

Cliffs Complete Study Editions

These easy-to-use volumes contain everything that a student or teacher needs for an individual classic. Each attractively illustrated volume includes abundant biographical, historical and literary background information. A descriptive bibliography provides guidance in the selection of additional reading.

The inviting three-column arrangement offers the maximum in convenience to the reader. Shakespeare's plays are presented in a full, authoritative text with modern spelling. Each line of Chaucer's original poetry is followed by a literal translation in simple current English. Adjacent to the complete text, there is a running commentary that gives clear supplementary discussion. Obscure words and allusions are keyed by line number and clarified opposite to where they occur.

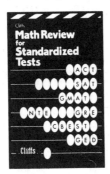
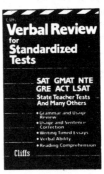

LET CLIFFS NOTES HELP YOU GET BETTER ACQUAINTED WITH THESE AUTHORS

■ ISAAC ASIMOV ■ TENNESSEE WILLIAMS ■ PLATO ■ F. SCOTT FITZGERALD ■ SHAKESPEARE ■ CHARLES DICKENS ■ GEORGE ELIOT ■ JANE AUSTEN ■ WILLA CATHER ■ WALT WHITMAN ■ ARTHUR MILLER ■ SALINGER ■ MACHIAVELLI ■ FRANZ KAFKA ■ EDGAR ALLEN POE ■ EDITH WHARTON ■ THOMAS SINCLAIR ■ PERCY SHELLEY JONATHON SWIFT ■ EMILY BRONTE ■ KATE CHOPIN ■ DANIEL DEFOE ■ DANTE ■ HENRY JAMES ■ WILLIAM FAULKNER ■ JAMES FENIMORE COOPER ■ MARK TWAIN ■ CHARLOTTE BRONTE ■ EDWARD ALBEE ■ ERNEST HEMINGWAY ■ JOHN STEINBECK ■ STEPHEN CRANE ■ GEORGE BERNARD SHAW ■ THOMAS HARDY ■ NATHANIEL HAWTHORNE ■ JAMES JOYCE ■ DOSTOEVSKY

GET CLIFFS NOTES

Cliffs Notes are America's most widely used study aids for literature. More than 200 titles are available covering well-known poems, plays and novels. Each provides expert analysis and background of plot, characters and author, in a way which can make the most difficult assignments easier to understand.

Available at your bookseller or order from Cliffs Notes.

See back cover for complete title listing.

P.O. Box 80728
Lincoln, NE 68501